Spread happiness everywhere :)

Isabelle ♡

KYLP

Spread happiness everywhere you go!
:)

Adventure to Autism Planet

by

Isabelle K. Mosca

with Illustrations by Kyle J. Mosca

COMTEQ
PUBLISHING
MARGATE, NEW JERSEY

Published by:
  ComteQ Publishing
  A division of ComteQ Communications, LLC
  101 N. Washington Ave. • Suite 2B
  Margate, New Jersey 08402
  609-487-9000 • Fax 609-487-9099
  Email: publisher@ComteQpublishing.com
  Website: www.ComteQpublishing.com

ISBN 9-781-935232-36-0
Library of Congress Control Number: 2011920554

Book & cover design by Jackie Caplan and Rob Huberman

CPSIA Section 103(a) Compliant
www.beaconstar.com/consumer
ID: K0115420 Tracking No: K0412207 - 7400
Printed in China
10 9 8 7 6 5 4 3 2 1

Isabelle stared dreamily into her aquarium at Zac and Vanessa, her new goldfish. They seemed to be yawning along with her as night shadows fell outside. She reached up for the fish food on her bedroom shelf, and quickly met hands with her eight-year-old twin brother Kyle.

"Mine!" he whined, grabbing the container.

"No, Kyle!" Isabelle snapped, barely yanking back the food out of his grasp.
"You always feed them too much! No!"

"Nnnnoooo! Kyle is frustrated!" he yelled, pulling on his own curly red hair, stomping his feet, then running from the room, sobbing.

Kyle was diagnosed with autism at age two, a disorder that affects the way children learn to speak or make friends, and often causes them to obsess on certain things. Isabelle especially did not like the way Kyle hogged the television remote and HAD to rewind everything he watched.

Once, he lined up all of her toys in a path all the way down the stairs and out the door! Kyle insisted that things in his room be arranged a certain way, and if they were not, he would freak out!

Not all boys were like this, Isabelle thought. Some of the other kids she met at the autism support group meetings had brothers and sisters with autism, but she felt funny talking to them about it.

Isabelle did not remember a time when her brother was not the way he was. That was just being Kyle. They did everything together, and had a special connection that only twins share. She found it easy to speak for her brother back then – when he could not find the words. Even in family photos they looked like any other family – smiling on the carousel, laughing down the slide, or hugging under the Christmas tree.

They read books and jumped on beds together. Kyle even wiped her tears when she cried.

Nowadays, Isabelle just wanted her brother to talk and tell her why he liked to draw movie logos all day long, and what was so great about rewinding the TV.

She was sitting on her bed listening to her favorite music CD when Kyle burst into her room with his hands cupped over his ears.

"No music, Isabelle! No music!" he begged.

Sometimes loud music bothered his ears. Isabelle felt the anger well up in her until she could not stop it. "Why can't you be – *normal?*" she blurted out.

Kyle cried, walking backwards out her door as she slammed it.

"Isabelle, are you okay?" Kyle asked from the other side of the door.

No response; just muffled sobs…

The next morning, Isabelle awoke to a loud crash, and then a thud. She rubbed her eyes and stirred gently.

THUD! THUD! CRASH! THUD!

"C'mon, Isabelle. Wake up, or you will be late for your flying umbrella lessons," Kyle exclaimed cheerily.

Flying lessons? Umbrellas? Isabelle rubbed her eyes. She sat straight up in her bed, realizing that this looked like her bedroom. But even after her focusing her eyes, the room's colors were still crayon-like and vibrant. Looking up towards Kyle's voice as she stepped onto the floor, her feet failed to hold her and she landed flat on her face.

You see, Kyle was *FLYING AN UMBRELLA* above her bed!

"Isabelle, get up and get dressed or you will miss your turn," he said so matter-of-factly, floating back to the floor to hand her a pink painted parasol with a parrot's head carved on the handle – her very own "flying machine."

No words came to her lips. She felt as if some giant vacuum cleaner were sucking up and scrambling her words as quickly as she tried to spit them out. Some words disappeared completely!

"Uhh, home – this – not – is, uh, Kyle…this is not – not – not home, Kyle. Are we…uhh, … Are – we – WHERE?" she asked, as Kyle gingerly helped her up from the floor.

"Welcome to Autism Planet," said Kyle. "This is the place those of us with autism go when you think we are not listening. We just have a different way of thinking, and we decided it was time to let one of you 'normal people' come and see for yourself. I'm so glad it is you, Isabelle."

Kyle seemed so much more "normal" here, she thought. No, maybe that was not the word for it. Now, *she* seemed to be the one who was having trouble expressing herself. *Gosh, it was so frustrating,* thought Isabelle, although she tried not to say so out loud.

"I am more 'normal' here, as you might say," Kyle told her, "but we think *normal* is not how you measure people. We are all so different, and the world would be so boring if we were all normal."

Isabelle tried to motion to Kyle in sign language to express the word, "think."

"Yes, we can read minds," he explained, "and do so many cool things — like fly with umbrellas, make air paintings and books with our fingers, go to school underwater, sing opera at the zoo, ride waterslides in the bathtub, and do whatever we imagine! Believe it, and it is possible!"

"C'mon, try the changing machine I invented," he offered.

Isabelle opened the closet door, and there, just like the pictures Kyle drew every day at home, were five glass stalls with dressed mannequins under lights, and a lever to pull when you make a clothing selection.
This was better than a candy machine! she thought.

Isabelle stepped into the cyclone (Kyle loved cyclones and twisters!) and her outfit wrapped up around her like a blanket. Kyle pressed a remote and he replayed it two more times just for the fun of it.

"I couldn't resist," he giggled so loud that Isabelle began to laugh, too.

"Where to?" Kyle asked.

"Uuh..Everywhere," Isabelle responded with joy. Their imagination was all that they needed to bring with them.

They spent the entire day flying with butterflies, jumping over fountains of ice cream, eating vegetables flavored with marshmallows and chocolate, sliding down rainbows, swinging along jungle vines, and talking about things they had never been able to share in the "normal" world.

Isabelle's adventure to Autism Planet gave her the chance to see their friends with autism in a whole new way.

Briana, who loved to swim, collect catalogues and dance, had created a lovely ladybug farm, complete with amusements and a tea party for all to share. Isabelle thought the tea party was the most fun.

Tim E. enjoyed showing off his homemade video games that were played without equipment. You just became a part of the game yourself. He challenged Isabelle and Kyle to a game of "Flying Farm Animals."

Isabelle had such a wonderful day hanging out with her twin brother and seeing life from his point of view.

The twins snuggled in to rest on an especially fluffy cloud.

"Kyle, I wish things could be just like this back on Earth," Isabelle said sadly.

"Do not be sad," he comforted. "This place is where we go in our heads when life gets too hard for us. It can be a restful place of joy, love and peace, too," Kyle insisted, fluffing up a section of cloud.

Isabelle yawned and nestled in as he continued.

"From time to time the world gets to be too much for those of us with autism, so we escape to here. But we don't want you to feel sorry for us.

We want you to accept us, just the way we are and know how much we appreciate you helping us, even when we don't look like we are listening to you," Kyle said, wiping away a tear from Isabelle's cheek.

"We are listening to you in our own special way."

"Please remind others to stop and say 'hello.'

"Don't give up on us – we don't give up on you!"

Isabelle closed her eyes. She was so amazed at Kyle's words. He spoke from the heart and made her feel so good about being his sister…

"Isabelle, are you alright?" Kyle asked.

Suddenly, Isabelle felt different and she opened her eyes. "Yes, Kyle, I'm alright," she answered.

"Sorry, Isabelle." Kyle was now standing at the foot of her bed, holding two chocolate frosted doughnuts in his hands. That's when she realized that they were back home, and she did not even need to click her heels once!

"There is no reason for you to be sorry, Kyle," she answered. "I am the one to say 'sorry' to you. I promise to be nicer to you from now on! Come on, let's go feed the fish together."

Isabelle grinned a knowing grin, and Kyle gave her a big squeeze.

THE END

Dear Reader:

Kyle and I do things together and separately. He likes to play basketball, draw lots of pictures and visit the thrift store with Daddy. I like to play with my friends, practice cheerleading and play softball.

Together, we love music and dancing, so we are in the school choir. We get to wear these cool robes to the concerts! We also like to go kayaking and canoeing with our family and friends. When this book is published, Kyle and I will be in sixth grade, so we are continuing to discover new ways to connect with each other.

If you know someone who is a little different, here are some ways you can be helpful and friendly.

Please say "hello." Don't you feel great when your friends say "hello"? Take the time, and you might make someone's day better.

Find something you have in common. Do you like the same music? TV show? Game? This is a great way to start a friendship.

Be patient. Maybe a kid does not talk because he or she does not know what to say, or is shy.

Invite them to play with you. Include them in sports, at lunch, and during recess. Everyone needs a friend to make them laugh and smile.

If you have a story about being a friend, you can tell it, too! I would love to hear it.

Peace, Love & Autism!

Isabelle

Kyle draws dozens of pictures each day, mostly portraits of his favorite TV and movie characters. He prefers crayons, markers, and sidewalk chalk. Kyle collects VHS and DVDs of his favorite films and draws many movie production company logos. His work has been on display at local art shows, and he is thrilled to see his drawings in this book! Kyle loves Spongebob, dancing, baseball, basketball, singing in choir, summer camp, youtube, and going to plays – especially musicals. Kyle would love to see your pictures and stories.

You can send them to the email address on the next page.

Isabelle is a lover of anything High School Musical related, as you might have noticed by the names of her goldfish. She also has a cat named Starsky. These days, she is a big Justin Bieber fan. It is her dream to appear on "The Today Show" and "The Ellen De Generes Show." Isabelle's idol is Temple Grandin, PhD., whose biography was the subject of an HBO Emmy award-winning movie.

Isabelle has read her book in her school on "Blow Bubbles 4 Autism" Day each year in April (which is Autism Awareness Month) over the last few years, and each time the kids are so moved by her story that she receives many letters of praise.

You can write Isabelle a letter, too. She keeps a special journal full of the letters in her room.

You can email either of the twins, or ask more about "Blow Bubbles 4 Autism" Day at:

welcometoautismplanet@yahoo.com

FACES

Autism is a neurological disorder which effects a person's ability to communicate, respond to their surroundings, and make friends. Sometimes their unusual behaviors make it very difficult for others to reach them. It affects one in 91 children in the USA, according to researchers from the Centers for Disease Control and Prevention and the Health Resources and Services Administration. There is no cure. Families try all kinds of therapies, but there is no one answer right now.

If you know someone with autism, try to find out what they like and see what you have in common. Maybe it is as easy as blowing bubbles together! There is a photo on page 30 in the book of Kyle and Isabelle's third grade class on **Blow Bubbles 4 Autism Day**. The event was started in Kyle's class in 2004, and now people all over the country "Blow Bubbles 4 Autism" in April.

Email FACES on bubbles4autism@yahoo.com to get your school involved.

People need to learn more about autism and to celebrate the gifts that it offers. When you are part of a group, it makes you happier, and it makes you feel good inside. Be a friend to someone with autism. If you would like more information on autism, ask your teacher, your parents or visit the web sites below.

These are national and state organizations with information:
www.autismspeaks.org
www.autismnj.org

Here is the **FACES Autism Support Network** web site where you can find the latest on my mom's autism support group and on "Blow Bubbles 4 Autism:"

www.faces-autismsupport.org

Each year, we try to break the Guinness World Record for "People in Multiple Venues Simultaneously Blowing Bubbles for One Minute." If you would like to join us, go to our Facebook page at "Blow Bubbles 4 Autism" or email us at:

bubbles4autism@yahoo.com

Or visit the FACES web site to get the forms and information you need. Get started in your school or business! We need 37,000 people to break the record, so please help us raise autism awareness and money for autism programs.

Acknowledgments

Isabelle and Kyle are donating a portion of the proceeds from the sale of this book to FACES Autism Support Network.

Special thanks to our wonderfully supportive friends and family; our dear friends at FACES; the faculty and students at Ventnor schools including Mrs. V, Mrs. Ricciotti, Mrs. DeSouza, Mrs. Walker, Mrs. Brahmi, Jose, William, Daniel, John, Bianca, Megan, Morgaine, Nina, Mikalena, Gianna, and Aila; the Marks, Mosca, Walton, Kelly, Elmer, and Devaney families; filmmaker Keri Bowers, Sheila Boyle, Patricia Durante, Cindy Lisowski, and our talented contributing photographer Crystal Posser-Craver.

We also wish to thank Atlantic City Electric, Ocean City Home Bank, The Polar Bear Run/Walk for Autism in Sea Isle City, The Donny Fund, Medical Explorer Post #147, Jersey Shore Parrothead Club, Temple Grandin, William Stillman, and all of our loyal Bubbles Day schools and business sponsors across the country. As Chris Devaney says, "It's all about the gifts and talents."

We are in your debt.

The Mosca Family

"Always presume intellect."

William Stillman, Author and Adult Self-Advocate with Asperger's Syndrome

"I can remember the frustration of not being able to talk. I knew what I wanted to say, but I could not get out the words, so I would just scream."

Temple Grandin, PhD, Author, Lecturer, and Self-Advocate with Autism